GW00383637

10 Second

Sermons

... and even quicker illustrations

10 Second Sermons

... and even quicker illustrations

Milton Jones

DARTON·LONGMAN +TODD

First published in 2011 by
Darton, Longman and Todd Ltd
1 Spencer Court
140 – 142 Wandsworth High Street
London SW18 4JJ

Reprinted 2011, 2012 twice

© 2011 Milton Jones

The right of Milton Jones to be identified as the author of this
work has been asserted in accordance with the Copyright,
Designs and Patents Act 1998.

ISBN: 978-0-232-52882-4

A catalogue record for this book is available from the
British Library
Printed and bound in Great Britain by Page Bros,
Norwich, Norfolk.

Contents

Introduction

Hello. As I try to pass around these tiny parcels, I hope the music stops long enough for you to unravel a layer. The prize is definitely worth having, so don't be put off by clumsy wrapping. Oh, and best hold them loosely ...

Thanks

... to all the those who have stopped and offered me directions – I may have lost you after a couple of sentences, but often followed you home for long enough to get somewhere I'd never have got to otherwise.

Here we go

We need to get away from religious clichés –
Amen?

And I'm quite prepared for you to say what
you want to about my faith as long as I can say
what I like about your lack of it.

The trick is to always start off with the right typeface....

Christianity is like a Cornish pastie. There's something in it, but sometimes it's difficult to find out what it is exactly.

Christianity is like knitting. Basically good, but appears to be responsible for a lot of bad things.

Some people think Christianity is like a mosquito – if you get infected you could turn into a gibbering wreck.

If being a Christian is just about trying to be like Jesus on your own, you may as well be an Elvis impersonator.

There are lots of Jesus impersonators, of course. Unfortunately most of us are still only part-time.

Christianity has done a lot of harm in the world, but only in the way that some men who wear certain football kits get into trouble – it doesn't mean they're actually part of the team!

People like Jesus because he hung around with drunks and prostitutes. So how come when I do that ...?

Now Jesus had a beard and sandals and long hair, although we don't know for sure about the long hair or the beard.
Or the sandals.

But like Bob Dylan and Tony Blair some people preferred the early stuff. The promise of revolution. And then – when it all appeared to go wrong – they felt tricked.

As we know, Jesus was a very humble man who said 'I am God'!

Visitors to a church often find themselves
thinking 'What am I doing here?' Sometimes
so do the members.

The early church had everything in
common, but now somehow parts of the
church have almost nothing in common with
anyone!

Ultimately, a church is just a rope bridge
made out of spaghetti.
Binoculars to watch a sunset.
A tiger in a polythene bag.

Sometimes people think of church as being like a giant helicopter. They don't want to get too close in case they get sucked into the rotas.

Others think of it as a Winnie the Pooh pyjama suit. Safe and warm, but they hope to goodness no one sees them in it.

And to some it's a baseball bat. For most of the time they play a nice little game with their friends. Then once a year they go out into the High Street and hit someone over the head with it.

Perhaps religion was just a phase God went through as well.

Of course, there are bound to be some conflicts of interests when you're part of a self-help group for unselfishness.

Some people say 'I really want to be used!' But if you ask them to put the chairs out they say 'Now I'm just being used!'

The Church is sometimes referred to as the Bride of Christ. Well, she must have a lovely personality.

You don't have to be part of a team. You can go and kick a ball around in a field on your own if you want. Just have a plan for when the opposition turn up, that's all.

Going to church should be like walking to the edge of the Grand Canyon and saying '… Ah!'

Church is a bit like being a member of a gym. Some people like the idea of going but don't. Others go, but aren't really training for anything. And some actually use it to help them with the race they're running.

A perfect church would be a community of hermits.

Church should be everyone arriving with one piece of the jigsaw.

If you're on a journey: in the same way that the services are not the motorway, a church is not the services.

Once I went to a seminar on coping with being single. But I was the only one who turned up. Which was good in a way.

What businessman would buy shares in a company with the Church's corporate image – ancient buildings in permanent disrepair, staffed by madmen and perverts, who sell bland nostalgia and dogmatic nonsense to a bunch of repressed misfits, most of whom just seem to need a jolly good slap?

Why don't you turn to the person next to you and say... 'this is really embarrassing isn't it'?

Salvation

Salvation is like being returned to factory settings. But you have to admit there is a factory, and that there could be some settings.

An Announcement

Would the owner of the
Ferrari number plate

CSG 3P71

please sell your car and
give the money to the poor.

Christians

Some Christians are like pens that only work sometimes. This makes you just want to throw them in the bin!

Others are like a large immobile man in a football shirt who's always shouting about what the team should be doing, but would be horrified to have to kick a ball himself.

If you want to persecute a lot of Christians, all you have to do is to ask them their star sign!

Christians can laugh longer and louder because they believe that it will all make sense in the end.

If being a Christian is only about *not* doing certain things, then that's a bit like a celebrity chef who is more famous for his allergies and intolerances.

There *has* to be more to being a Christian than just being quite nice.

We are all unique...

The word 'gospel' means good news. But today it's more a type of music. So when Jesus said we should go into all the world and preach the gospel he didn't mean we had to dress up as Aretha Franklin. I know that now.

The gospel is like a cheese and gherkin sandwich. But some people don't like the taste of the gherkin of repentance. But without the gherkin it's not really a cheese and gherkin sandwich, is it?

Repentance is like an antibiotic. You have to take it every day until you finish the course.

ospel

To say that Christianity is just one of several religions is a bit like saying that water is just one of many types of drink – it's a bit more fundamental than that.

people who talk about 'good news'

people who actually are good news

Authority

To have authority, you have to *be* the message. Like Jamie Oliver, Lady Gaga and Father Christmas.

Sin

Something's wrong with the world. It's like a chocolate cake that has fallen face down on the floor of a chicken coop. So you either sweep the whole lot away, or try and rescue as much as you can.

People think of the concept of sin as being repressive and restrictive. And it's true – you can drive a car a lot faster if you have no brakes.

Who was it who said that brilliant thing about being conceited? Oh yes, it was me ….

Persistent niggling sin is a bit like leaving the car glove compartment light on. Slowly it saps all the energy so that eventually you can't get going at all.

Gossip

Gossip is bullying people who're not there.

Jealousy

Jealousy is desperately wanting another person's gifts, but the fantasy never seems to include not having your own.

Anger

Anger is making your feelings about an 'injustice' more important than the possible injustice of other people having to listen to them.

Lust

Lust is rehearsing for a play
in which you shouldn't have a part.

Sloth

Sloth is being determined to
get to grips with all three deadly sins.

Greed

Greed is seeing if the grass is greener
on the other side of your appetite –
in the end it's usually just your face
that goes that colour.

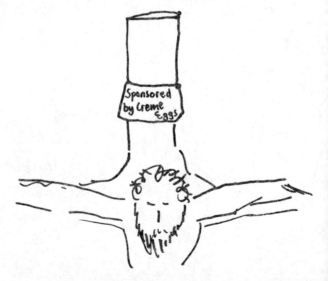

Evil

No-one thinks they are evil.
In fact most really evil people think
they are doing good.

The Bible

You'd never get the Bible published today, of course – you'd have to make it into a film first. Call it *Three Wise Men and a Baby* or *My Big Fat Greek Testament* – starring Leonardo di Caprio as Jesus, Angelina Jolie as Mary Magdalene and the voice of Eddie Murphy as the talking donkey. The book would have pictures from the film and you'd have to call it *The Dummies Guide to Religion* or *The Where's Jesus Book*.

Perhaps people are suspicious of the Bible because Christians sometimes try to use it to win arguments with people who don't know anything about it. Which is a bit like being lost in London and someone saying to you 'Well if I could just refer you to the *A to Z*, page 27, grid reference G4 ....'

Its Moses coming down the mountain with what look like swimming floats. We must be going back across the Red Sea again!

The Bible should be read carefully. For instance, recently I found out that a lot of the Ten Commandments have the word 'not' in them! I wish I'd known that earlier.

There are lots of versions of the Bible. AV, NIV, RSV … The easiest to use is the PVC version – you just stretch it to say whatever you want it to.

You have to remember that the Bible is often a translation of someone trying to communicate the indescribable.

Noah

Of course flood stories occur in
many cultures, but none are trivialised
quite as much as in Christianity.

Adam

Well, it's not as if his parents could have
bailed him out.

Eve! Whatever you do
use fig leaves,
not nettles!

Five Loaves

The other miracle at the Feeding of the Five Thousand is that only one person there had any food. Or so they said.

Perhaps some people are reluctant to give up their two fish and five loaves today because they've been in the Church long enough to know that by next week they could be in charge of the whole of the hospitality ministry for Western Europe.

nd Two Fish

God

What kind of an almighty God couldn't make the world in seven days?

Some people think of God as a doddery old man who can't hear properly and when someone said to him 'Are you alright?', he said 'What, let there be light? Oh dear, what have I done!'

Others see him like a cruel gardener who says to children 'Come and play in my garden with the trees and the grass and the land mines.'

Perhaps God's more like a beautiful Italian woman who knows just how to make your favourite spaghetti sauce. But don't cheat on her otherwise she'll throw it all over you.

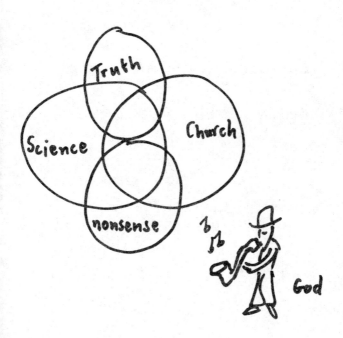

Or like a driving instructor whose last words as he jumps out of the car are 'I tell you – it's not a drive-thru McDonald's!'

I think God is like Mozart, and we are the notes.

God is the AA, and we are the breakdowns.

God is Calvin Klein. We are pants.

Grace

Grace is fantastic when *you* receive it, but can be strangely annoying when you see others benefiting from it, especially if they seem to have had more fun than you in the meantime. *I* may have got through the traffic lights in the nick of time, but what about the others who got through after me? Surely the policeman will throw the book at them? *They* were definitely in the wrong. But what's this? He lets them off with a warning. And a hug!? Hang on a minute ....

The Voic

So then I bandaged his wounds
and then he said - 'there's something
different about you...'

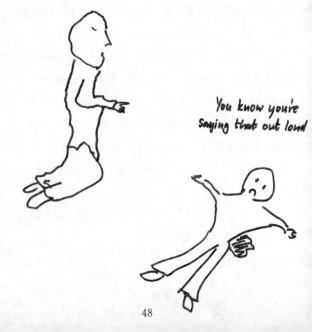

You know you're
saying that out loud

# of God

Today there are plenty of madmen saying that God has told them things. Some of them are drunk in the High Street, while others are leading countries.

Hearing God's voice is often like trying to hear a satnav that you've locked in the boot of your car because you thought you wouldn't need it.

Being guided by God is a bit like walking. If you stand still on one leg at any one point you will probably fall over. But if you keep moving, over the course of time you'll make progress in the right direction.

Forgiveness

Once I had a really good book about forgiveness. But I lent it to a friend and they lost it. They're not my friend any more.

Doubt

We all have doubts. Why should we accept the Bible? How does that sin-faith-resurrection equation work scientifically? And what is it with Christians who wear both socks and sandals? Some things are just a mystery.

The story of the man who didn't listen to parables... sorry I haven't really thought this through

Faith

My faith is like a joke – some people get it and some people don't, and some people pretend they get it, and some people pretend they don't.

Faith is like standing still in the noise, knowing that the bus is coming. And occasionally, through the fog and the traffic, catching a glimpse of something big and red.

Some of the others waiting might give up. Or decide they can make the journey on their own. Or that there is no journey – that the bus stop is all there is: a bench and a shelter, with a single training shoe lying on the roof – it's just the way things are ....

If you spend too long in prison you can become institutionalised, and it can be difficult to make that leap of faith over the wall to freedom. This applies to being locked up in church culture too.

Peace is knowing the reason not to be
frightened by the facts this time.

Christmas

The arrival of Jesus signifies the end of the keeping of traditions for the sake of tradition. Perhaps he shouldn't have come at Christmas then.

Sometimes I feel like Joseph at the inn in Bethlehem holding a crib of straw and saying 'No, I asked to see the manager!'

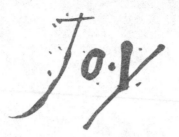

Joy is to be so sure that the facts of a situation don't fit the reality that you can't help sniggering.

Patience is just looking at the situation from Google Earth occasionally.

Goodness

If goodness is to be 'of God', then a good person can expect to be 'not believed in' by most people most of the time.

'Sell your possessions and give the money to the poor...'

Best of 3?

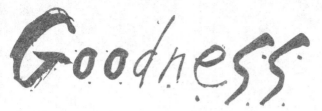

Faithfulness

Faithfulness is sticking with a story that's difficult to understand because you've read other books by the same author.

Hope

Perhaps hope is like ordering something on Amazon. Every so often you get little messages saying 'It's on its way'. Then one day the doorbell will ring! But if you don't answer, your hope might disappear to the depot for ever and ever.

Encouragement

Just saying 'I really want to encourage you' isn't an encouragement at all!

Love

Everyone can be either wonderful or really annoying if you think about them long enough.

The Holy

The Spirit of God is a real person you can invite in. But watch out – in time he will go over to the fridge, pull it from the wall and say 'What's all this mess under here?' But at least he helps clear up.

Some people are afraid of the Holy Spirit because they think it might be like a ghost in an episode of *Scooby Doo* who turns out to be Mr Robinson the janitor after all.

Spirit

The Holy Spirit is like a good spy who can get information and arrange explosions behind enemy lines. An unexpected friend in a difficult place. But no one knows how he does it. As soon as the code is discovered it gets changed.

Judgement will be like being on a luggage carousel – eventually you will get claimed by your rightful owner.

At that last moment we will all be turned from feather dusters into Dysons, and everyone will be able to see just how much good we have done.

On that day we will suddenly see our judgment for what it really was. You might think you're okay but sometimes it's difficult to see what you're hanging on to. Again, that book would have been really useful here.

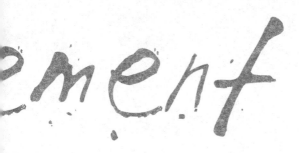

It will be as if you are asleep and the phone rings. Suddenly you will realise that all along there has been a different reality.

Like the dustman, he will arrive on a day you're not expecting. To sort the rubbish from the recyclable.

Christians sometimes speak about their faith with the over-certainty of someone getting their facts straight before making a dodgy insurance claim.

Leadership

We all agree that manipulation is a bad thing. Let me hear you say 'Yes!'

The Good Shepherd lays down his life for the sheep. The Bad Shepherd lays down his wife for the sheep.

Weak leadership results in the bland leading the bland.

I have three points this morning....

Communicating

Hang on....
is this for your
benefit or ours?

Christians sometimes shout 'Once I was dead but now I'm alive!' But then so do zombies.

Look, if I'm honest, when I talk to people about God, 14% is from personal experience, 23% is other peoples' experience and 84% is hopeless exaggeration. It may be even more.

If you get tangled up in Christian words you risk becoming one of those parts of the vine who lose their saltiness and therefore cannot finish the race.

From the outside there's a fine line between being different to everyone else, and just being a weirdo.

The biggest question many Christians are asking the world today is 'Will you give us some money to help pay for our new roof?'

Denominations

We all have different favourite bits of the same story.

I used to believe in evolution. But then one day I joined a Baptist church and I could tell I was going to have to adapt in order to survive!

Yeah, and if you're an Anglican and you don't like what I'm saying, think of me like a godparent at one of your christenings. I may have told you a pack of lies but at least you'll never see me again!

The Devil

So here we are then, apparently caught
between the deep blue sea and a little red
imaginary man with a goatee beard, eating
his very own devilled chicken and devil's
chocolate fudge cake.

But if he's imaginary who is it who keeps
saying 'The grass is always greener', 'You
can fly this plane on your own if you want'
and 'Don't worry, the eject button only
applies to the CD player'?

Holiness

I've been a christian for 40 years

Holy means set apart. Not like a set of cutlery that only comes out on Sundays. More like a Swiss army knife – remove a splinter, cut a rope, open a bottle, anytime anywhere. Whatever the boss needs.

How come you're still not very nice?

The Alternatives

Over the course of a lifetime we will all attend a few surprise parties, but just the one surprise funeral.

You might think you've collected lots of daisies, but what if it turns out you were actually on a rugby pitch and there was a match going on? Or you thought you were in a rugby match and all along you were supposed to be collecting daisies? Maybe life isn't what you thought it was about?

'Fame and her handmaidens are but fleeting.'

Anon

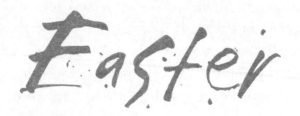

Easter

Sometimes religion can seem like the last person in a long game of Chinese whispers. Once Jesus said 'Love God and each other', and now we have the Easter Bunny!

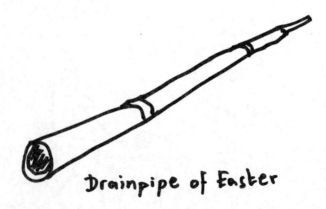

Drainpipe of Easter

Weddings

Of course, Jesus was a guest at a wedding in Canaan. Although the number of times this is mentioned at weddings, he might be regretting it now.

Heaven

Heaven will be good. Very good.
A new start, a better chocolate cake and all
from the perspective of Google Universe.

Obviously I don't know exactly what
Heaven will be like, but all I can say is I
wouldn't want to be John Lennon.

I think Heaven will be like coming home to
a surprise party after a bad day.

Hell

Hell will not be good in any way.

In Hell, everyone who has spent their life trying to avoid God will get to do it permanently. But in that moment they will also suddenly realise the source of everything good.

And finally

A world without God is a book without a plot.
A curry without taste.
A life without a purpose.

But in the end we are all mice listening to
    Mozart.
Elephants reading Braille.
Bats watching snooker.

But like science, fashion and jazz, just
because I might not understand it, doesn't
mean it doesn't exist.

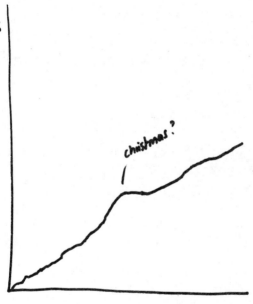

weirdness

christmas?

hours spent
in church meetings

Words are not enough. Or pictures.